PRÍBEH ČÍSIEL

THE NUMBER STORY

SMALL BOOK ONE

ENGLISH – SLOVAK

---

*Numbers Teach Children
Their Number Names*

written and illustrated by

MISS ANNA

Early Reader Edition of *The Number Story 1*
Bronze Medal Winner, 2016 Wishing Shelf Book Award

Cover by | Lumpy Publishing
Layout by | Lumpy Publishing
Translated by Petra Kamenárová
Coloring by Jieeun Woo and Maria Mirabella

Library of Congress Control Number: 2018902040

Names: Miss Anna, author.
Title: Number story : numbers teach children their number names / Miss Anna.
Description: Portland, OR: Lumpy Publishing, 2018.
Identifiers: ISBN 978-1-945977-48-0 | LCCN 2018902040
Summary: The pictures and rhymes present stories which introduce numbers 0-10.
Subjects: LCSH Numeration—English--Slovak--Pictorial works--Juvenile literature. | BISAC JUVENILE NONFICTION /
Languages: English--Slovak
Classification: LCC QA141.3 .M57 2018 | DDC 513—dc23

Publisher: Lumpy Publishing
Website: www.missannabooks.com
Email: missanna@missannabooks.com

Paperback: ISBN 978-1-945977-48-0
Printed in the U.S.A.   1 3 5 7 9 10 8 6 4 2

Chceš sa naučiť čísla podľa ich mien?

It is very easy and a lot of fun!

Je to ľahké a plné zmien!

Say-along our little jingle

Zaspievajme si spolu túto pesničku.

starting from Number One!

Začneme s číslom jeden.

ONE   looks like my one finger.

JEDEN

Vyzerá ako môj jeden prstík.

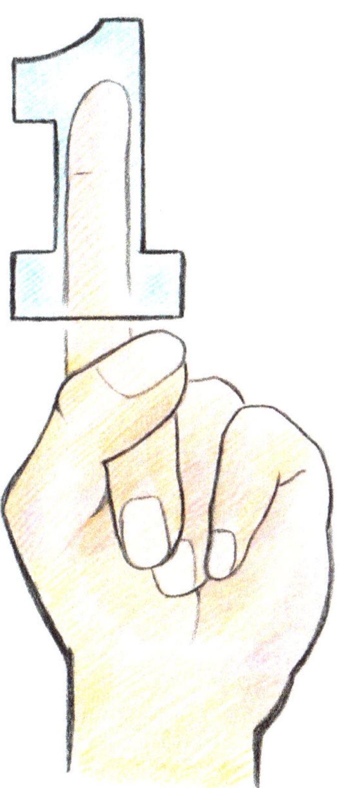

ONE!

JEDNA!

2

TWO trails a tail.

DVA

Má chvostík.

A TAIL! CHVOSTÍK!

3

THREE has bumps.

TRI

Je ako kopec.

BUMPY! KOPEC!

4

FOUR carries a sail.

ŠTYRI

Je to plachetnica.

4
PLACHTÍ!
A SAIL!

5

FIVE   is a racing track.

PÄŤ

Je to závodná dráha.

VROOM
BRRRM !

SIX curves like a snail.

ŠESŤ

Ohýba sa ako slimák.

A SNAIL! SLIMÁK!

7

SEVEN has a sharp angle.

SEDEM
Má ostré hrany.

OUCH!
AU!

8

E I G H T   is rollercoaster rails.

OSEM

Je ako horská dráha.

JÉÉJ!
YIPPEE!

NINE is a bubble on a stick.

DEVÄŤ

Je ako bublina.

A BUBBLE! BUBLINA!

10

TEN   is an eye of a whale.

DESAŤ

Je ako jedno očko.

HELLO! HALLÓ!

And A
O
ZERO is an empty pail.

NULA
Je prázdne vedierko.

IT'S EMPTY!
Je prázdne!

Thank you for playing with us today.

We had a lot of fun too!

Ďakujem, že ste sa dnes hrali s nami.

Tiež sme sa bavili!

We are your Number friends,
Zero to Ten,
Who will be here for you~
Sme kamaráti s Vami
Z nuly do desať!
Budeme tu pre Vás~

Bye-bye now!
See you again soon!
Dovidenia, na teraz!
Vidíme sa čoskoro!

The Numbers are *SINGING* too!

To sing-a-long, look for Miss Anna Number Story
at your favorite music store like iTUNES.

MP3

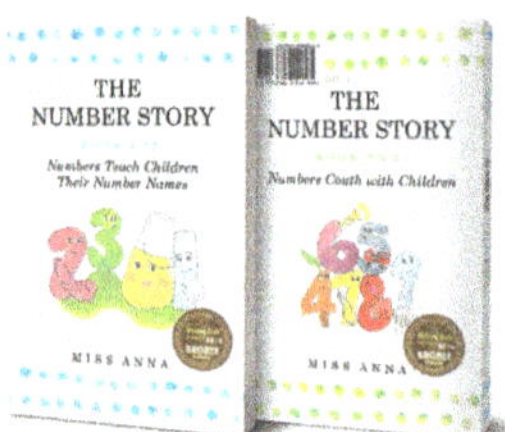

Numbers 0-10
IDENTIFYING
& COUNTING

Number Story 1 & 2
isbn: 978-0-996216-48-7

Numbers 11-20
& Ordinals

first, second, third...

Number Story 3 & 4
isbn: 978-1-945977-01-5

Numbers 0-100
& Place Values

ones, tens, hundreds...

Number Story 5 & 6
isbn: 978-1-945977-06-0

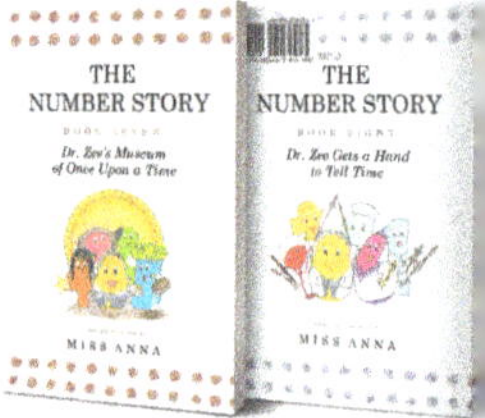

About Clocks
& Telling Time

hours, minutes, seconds...

Number Story 7 & 8
isbn: 978-1-949320-40-4

For more Miss Anna books to love,
visit us at

www.missannabooks.com

Numbers are working hard all over the world!
Come Travel the World with Us!